LEAD, DON'T SELF-SABOTAGE

*Navigating Leadership Pitfalls
in Social Entrepreneurship*

© 2023 by Vongai Nyahunzvi

All rights reserved. No part of this publication may be reproduced, stored in a retrieval system, or transmitted in any form or by any means—electronic, mechanical, photocopy, recording, scanning, or other—except for brief quotations in critical reviews or articles, without the prior written permission of the author.

Unless otherwise noted, the author and the publisher make no explicit guarantees as to the accuracy of the information contained in this book and in some cases, names of people and places have been altered to protect their privacy.

First Edition
ISBN: 9798851748851
Library of Congress Control Number:
This book was produced in the United Kingdom.

LEAD, DON'T SELF-SABOTAGE

*Navigating Leadership Pitfalls
in Social Entrepreneurship*

Dr. Vongai Nyahunzvi

DEDICATIONS

To my husband Studymore, I express my deepest love and gratitude. Your unwavering faith in my abilities, even in times of self-doubt, has been my anchor. You have been my confidante, my rock, and my partner in every sense. Your unconditional love has not just influenced my personal life, but it has also permeated my professional journey. Thank you for being my guiding light in the darkest of nights and my beacon of hope always.

To our precious children, Myles, Ethan, and Jude, you have brought unfathomable joy into my life. You've been my inspiration and my greatest motivators. Your constant curiosity, relentless energy, and unconditional love have often given me the perspective I needed to face my challenges. I dedicate this book to your dreams and aspirations, hoping that it becomes a stepping stone in your pursuit of greatness.

To Wendy Kopp, the best manager I ever had, a profound thank you. The opportunity you provided for continued experimentation has shaped my professional journey. Your faith in my ideas, your willingness to embrace the unconventional, and your tireless support have been instrumental in my growth. You have not only been a manager but a mentor, a leader, and a guiding star.

And to all the leaders I have had the honour of working with across the years, thank you. You have pushed me, challenged me, encouraged me, and above all, helped me evolve as a professional.

To the cherished ones in my life and the pillars of strength in my career, I extend my heartfelt gratitude. To all of you, my deepest appreciation. Your unwavering support and love have been the driving forces behind this accomplishment. This book would not have been possible without each and every one of you. Thank you for being part of my journey.

Vongai

CONTENTS

Dedications... 5
FOREWORD... 1
Preface.. 4
Introduction.. 7
Approval Addiction... 12
Lack of Self Awareness Syndrome................................ 23
Lone Ranger Syndrome.. 33
Founder Bias Syndrome... 43
Messiah Complex Syndrome.. 53
Superhero Syndrome.. 59
Compassion Fatigue... 69
Perfectionist Syndrome.. 81
Burn out syndrome... 92
Imposter Syndrome.. 102
Mission Drift... 113
Suggestions on leveraging this book.......................... 122

FOREWORD

I started out as a "social entrepreneur" before I'd ever heard that term. My now three-decades-long journey has afforded me the incredible opportunity to do meaningful work with kindred spirits who share my values and have pushed me every step of the way. It has exposed me to intense and engaging learning curves, on everything from addressing the roots of inequity to developing strong and sustainable organisations.

Perhaps the most intense learning curve of all has been an inner journey–involving my own self-exploration and development. It's an ongoing process, and one that will never be finished, involving deepening awareness of my conditioned patterns, building my connectedness and compassion for self and others, learning to show up in my full truth and vulnerability, and developing my ability to deeply listen and embrace a learning orientation.

Working with social entrepreneurs across sectors and across our global network, I've seen firsthand that this is a universal journey towards our most conscious, open states even amidst the trauma and urgency that swirls around us.

We couldn't have a more inspirational and wise guide than Vongai Nyahunzvi. She grew up experiencing and overcoming the most severe inequities our world has to offer, and has developed along the way deep wisdom, strength, and compassion. I feel so grateful for years of working in close partnership with her, and am so happy that she is sharing her gifts with the world through this book. *Lead, Don't Self-Sabotage* is invaluable in pulling together in one place the syndromes that hold back the best of us and the opportunities for reflection that can unlock our most conscious leadership.

Ultimately, none of us alone will shape the world we envision. It will take all of us exercising collective leadership towards peace, justice, and sustainability. This book will help us all in the journey towards practising leadership that in turn fosters the agency and leadership of all of us.

Wendy Kopp
CEO & Co-Founder, Teach For All

PREFACE

Every book has a soul, an intangible essence that is breathed into it by its creator. As the author of "*Lead, Don't Self Sabotage: Navigating Leadership Pitfalls in Social Entrepreneurship*", my hope is to make this book's soul a companion to you on your leadership journey.

Before we delve into the pages that follow, it's crucial to clarify the nature of the stories that serve as the backbone of this book. These stories are not direct accounts of real individuals, they embody common threads and themes that have emerged through my work in the leadership space. They represent shared human experiences, the joys, and pains, the triumphs and missteps that colour the tapestry of leadership, particularly within social entrepreneurship.

It's also important for you to know that while I may stand on this side of the pages as the author, I am simultaneously a traveller on the journey to better leadership. I've been in the trenches, and I continue to navigate my way, stumbling, learning, and growing, much like the characters in the stories. In fact, writing this book has been an exercise in introspection, and in some chapters, I found myself writing about my own struggles and revelations.

The choice to expose my own vulnerabilities and missteps was not an easy one, but it was necessary. As leaders, we often feel the pressure to appear invincible, to always have the answers. But true leadership, I've found, lies not in infallibility but in vulnerability, in the courage to admit when we're lost, and in the humility to learn and grow.

As you read this book, know that I do not claim to have all the answers. Instead, I offer you a lens through which to view leadership and its challenges, distilled from shared experiences and personal revelations. I invite you to approach this book not as a manual from an all-knowing author but as a conversation with a fellow traveller, one who has traversed similar paths, weathered similar storms, and continues to journey on.

With hope and humility, let's embark on this voyage of discovery together, charting a course toward more effective, empathetic, and resilient leadership in the realm of social entrepreneurship.

Let the journey begin.

Chapter 0

INTRODUCTION

For the past two decades, I've had the distinct honour of collaborating with social entrepreneurs from a broad range of backgrounds. In this enlightening journey, I have experienced the transformative influence of exceptional leadership and the profound effects it can generate. However, I have also observed how the lack or misdirection of effective leadership can crumble even the most hopeful ventures. Interestingly, leadership is often the element that is most often overlooked.

Social entrepreneurs are regularly met with numerous challenges including limited resources, shifting market trends, and the intricate nature of societal issues. Furthermore, they occasionally face internal obstacles that are self-created, often referred to as "self-sabotage". These can take the form of errors, mindsets, or actions that unintentionally compromise their goals. In this book we will refer to these as syndromes. Identifying and circumventing these 'self-inflicted' barriers is vital for the triumph and longevity of any social venture.

My hope as an author is that the chapters of this book will offer social entrepreneurs practical wisdom derived from fictional narratives, illuminating ways to overcome leadership pitfalls, thus enabling them to lead their ventures towards meaningful transformations.

"Lead, Don't Self-Sabotage: Navigating Leadership Pitfalls in Social Entrepreneurship" is a book committed to shedding light on the trials and triumphs these catalysts for change have faced.

Moreover, I acknowledge that the journey of social entrepreneurship intertwines personal and professional dimensions. Therefore, I have incorporated reflective narratives and advice on handling specific self-sabotage tendencies. This method aims to develop not just the skills, but also the mindset indispensable for impactful leadership.

Whether you are embarking on your social entrepreneurship journey, seeking to expand an existing venture, or aiming to instil a culture of impactful leadership within your organisation, this book will be relevant. I urge you to delve into the subsequent pages with an open heart and a dedication to continued self-exploration and enhancement.

As you navigate through the pages of this book, you will encounter a myriad of concepts, strategies, and insights about leadership. These ideas are meant to guide you, inspire you, and challenge your understanding of leadership in the context of social entrepreneurship. However, the real transformation happens when you internalise these concepts and apply them in your own leadership journey.

To aid you in this process, we have included a set of self-reflection questions at the end of each chapter. These questions are designed to help you delve deeper into the material, ponder its implications, and evaluate how you can incorporate these insights into your own practices. They will prompt you to introspect, to question, to affirm, and ultimately to grow as a leader. The self-reflection exercise is not a test, but an invitation for you to engage more intimately with the content of this book. You are encouraged to be honest and open in your responses. There are no right or wrong answers, only opportunities for learning and growth.

As you respond to these questions, remember that self-reflection is a personal and transformative process that requires time and patience. Allow yourself the freedom to explore your thoughts and feelings without judgement. Use this as an opportunity to understand your strengths, identify areas for improvement, and develop strategies to become a more effective leader.

Welcome to "Lead, Don't Self-Sabotage: Navigating Leadership Pitfalls in Social Entrepreneurship".

Chapter 1

APPROVAL ADDICTION

When the Pursuit of Applause Derailed a Leader's Journey

Nestled within the heart of Sierra Leone's lush countryside, a ray of hope was once born through the tireless efforts of a young, ambitious leader named Aminata Mensah. His social enterprise, Zawadi Initiative, aimed to uplift rural communities by providing access to education, microfinance, and healthcare.

Aminata was a visionary. Having grown up in a humble household, he had witnessed the shackles of poverty. His mission was deeply personal. The Zawadi Initiative quickly gained momentum, and Aminata's dedication seemed unshakeable.

As Zawadi flourished, so did Aminata's reputation. He began to receive invitations to speak at international conferences and garnered media attention. Recognition flowed in from every corner of the globe. Slowly, an insidious transformation began to take place. Aminata started craving validation and approval. His decisions began to be guided not by the needs of the communities he served, but by what would win him more accolades.

He started engaging in high-profile, media-attractive projects that had little impact on the ground but made for great headlines. One such project was a tech centre, which was not in line with the immediate needs of the community, who were struggling with basic healthcare and education.

As approval addiction consumed Aminata, the core team of Zawadi Initiative began to realise the disconnect between their leader's actions and the organisation's original mission. Amina, the head of community relations, confronted Aminata. She told him stories of how the villagers were suffering because the resources were being channelled into projects that didn't address their immediate needs. Aminata's reaction was one of denial and aggression. His addiction to approval had blinded him to such an extent that any critique felt like an attack on his identity.

As months went by, Zawadi Initiative's projects began to crumble. The communities felt betrayed. The media, which had once celebrated Aminata, began to highlight the organisation's failures.

In a twist of fate, Aminata was invited to a community gathering in a remote village. There, he saw the desperate eyes of the children who lacked educational resources, and the weary faces of women who struggled for basic healthcare. It was a reflection of his past, a reminder of his original mission.

The applause and awards felt hollow compared to the stark reality in front of him. Aminata, a broken man, realised the damage his approval addiction had caused. It was time for redemption, but this time, not for applause or accolades, but for the silent smiles of the very people he had vowed to serve.

The road to rebuilding the Zawadi Initiative was steep. Aminata stepped down as the leader, taking on a role where he could work closely with the communities. Amina took the helm, steering the organisation back to its roots.

Aminata Mensah's descent from the heights of acclaim was steep and turbulent, but now he had chosen a path of humility and service. It was a path strewn with regret and self-reflection, but also with the quiet strength of rediscovery.

Amina, the newly appointed leader of Zawadi Initiative, proved to be adept at steering the organisation back to its core values. With her firm yet empathetic approach, she began to rebuild the bridges that Aminata's approval addiction had burned. Meanwhile, Aminata devoted himself to the ground-level work. With a newfound humility, he listened more than he spoke, observing the intricate fabric of the community's needs. He started teaching in the local school, and soon, the community began to see the man he was before the applause had clouded his vision.

One day, a cultural festival was organised by the Zawadi Initiative to celebrate and preserve the local heritage. It was a vibrant event, with the air resounding with the melodies of traditional songs, and the ground beneath quaking from the rhythms of dances.

Aminata was asked to speak at the festival. As he stood on the stage, looking at the faces in the crowd, he felt a swell of emotions. This time, he didn't have a meticulously prepared speech aimed to impress. Instead, he spoke from his heart. He apologised for losing sight of what truly mattered and thanked the community for teaching him the essence of service and humanity. His words were simple but laden with genuine emotion.

In an unexpected moment, an elderly woman from the community, Mama Nia, stood up and began to sing a traditional song of forgiveness and unity. One by one, others joined in until the air was filled with a chorus that seemed to heal and unite.

Amina, who was watching from the sidelines, felt tears streaming down her face. This was what the Zawadi Initiative was all about - not just the tangible development but the binding of souls, the creation of harmony between aspirations and heritage. Under Amina's leadership, with Aminata's unwavering support, Zawadi Initiative began to thrive anew. The community was involved in every step, and transparent communication was emphasised.

Lessons from Approval Addiction

- ❖ The initial euphoria of recognition and applause can be intoxicating, but it's fleeting. Relying on it for self-worth or direction can lead to an insatiable and dangerous need for more.

- ❖ Seeking constant validation can cloud one's judgement, leading to decisions that prioritise personal acclaim over genuine impact or purpose.

- ❖ When addicted to approval, any critique or feedback can be perceived as a personal attack, leading to defensiveness and denial, rather than constructive action.

- ❖ The constant chase for external validation can lead to a loss of personal and professional authenticity. Actions and decisions become a reflection of what's popular or praiseworthy rather than what's genuinely needed or right.

- ❖ Realising the pitfalls of approval addiction and working towards rectifying mistakes can lead to redemption, but the path is often challenging and requires humility and genuine intent.

- ❖ True satisfaction and fulfilment come from recognising one's internal worth and the real impact of one's actions, rather than relying solely on external praise.
- ❖ It's essential to periodically reconnect with one's roots and initial purpose to prevent getting swayed by external factors and to maintain clarity in vision.

Overcoming Approval Addiction

1. Revisit Your 'Why'. Regularly reflect on the reason you started your venture. This grounding exercise can remind you of your true purpose and mission.
2. Seek Genuine Feedback. Establish a circle of trusted advisors, mentors, or peers who can provide honest and constructive feedback without the intent to flatter.
3. Limit Exposure. While staying informed is crucial, excessive exposure to social media or

platforms that focus on validation can skew perspectives. Set boundaries or designated times to check these platforms.

4. Celebrate Internal Milestones. Instead of only recognizing achievements that receive external validation, celebrate internal milestones like a successful team meeting, a well-executed strategy, or a personal growth moment.

5. Embrace Failure. Understand that not every endeavour will be successful, and that's okay. Embracing failure as a learning opportunity can reduce the constant need for external validation.

6. Limit Comparisons. Every social entrepreneur's journey is unique. Instead of comparing your achievements with others, focus on your path, your progress, and the difference you're making.

7. Cultivate Gratitude. Regularly express gratitude for what you have and the progress you've made. This can shift the focus from

seeking external validation to appreciating the intrinsic value of your journey.

Approval Addiction Self Reflection Questions

Take your time to reflect on these questions honestly. Remember, the goal is not to judge or chastise yourself, but to better understand your patterns and make a conscious effort to break free from the cycle of approval addiction.

1. What strengths or talents have I demonstrated in my work that I feel proud of, independent of external validation?
2. When have I felt most authentic in my role as a social entrepreneur, and what was I doing at that time?
3. What accomplishments in my journey have given me intrinsic satisfaction without needing acknowledgment from others?
4. How can I harness my existing skills and experiences to foster self-assurance and minimise the need for approval?

5. When have I noticed a disconnect between my actions and my initiative's core values due to external validation? How did this make me feel?
6. How might my decisions or strategies shift if I were completely free from the desire for external approval?
7. How does the fear of disapproval or rejection impact the choices I make for my social enterprise? What alternative choices could I make?
8. In seeking approval, have there been opportunities or collaborations I've missed or overlooked?

Chapter 2

LACK OF SELF AWARENESS SYNDROME

Mind the Gap

In this chapter I will share a story about Bisi, a social enterprise leader whose journey was marred by a lack of self-awareness. Bisi's tale serves as a reminder of the importance of knowing oneself and understanding the ripple effects of one's actions.

Bisi, an audacious and energetic woman from Burundi, harboured dreams as boundless as the skies. She sought to uplift her community, which, though brimming with culture, was beleaguered by poverty and educational disparities. Inspired to effect change, Bisi founded "Sankofa Foundation," a social enterprise aimed at empowering women and children through education and skills training.

Sankofa grew rapidly, with Bisi at the helm. The community lauded her efforts, and her passionate demeanour earned her recognition and grants. However, Bisi was steadfastly focused on the external facets of her leadership and her enterprise. The thought of introspection and understanding her inner self remained alien.

As Sankofa expanded, Bisi's decision-making grew increasingly impulsive and autocratic. She mistook her initial success as evidence of her infallibility. Sankofa, which was once a cohesive community endeavour, slowly began to morph into a manifestation of Bisi's unchecked ambitions.

The staff and beneficiaries of Sankofa began to feel the repercussions of Bisi's lack of self-awareness. Her inability to recognize the impacts of her actions led to strained relationships and a decline in organisational morale. In Bisi's eyes, she was merely pushing for excellence. However, in the eyes of others, she was inadvertently pushing people away.

One fateful day, a town hall meeting was convened by the elders and members of Sankofa. The air was thick with trepidation as individuals hesitantly began recounting their experiences. The once scattered whispers converged into a chorus that couldn't be ignored.

As Bisi listened, her first reaction was one of disbelief and defence. However, as the stories unfurled, something within her cracked. The enormity of her own unawareness began to weigh upon her. The realisation that she had strayed so far from her original mission was both haunting and humbling.

With guidance from elders and her community, Bisi embarked on a journey of self-discovery. She sought to understand the nuances of her behaviour and the way they shaped her environment. Through counselling, mentorship, and embracing feedback, she worked ardently to realign her internal compass.

Months later, a reformed Bisi stood before her community. Her eyes, once blazing with unchecked fervour, now sparkled with wisdom and humility. Sankofa Foundation underwent a renaissance as Bisi's newfound self-awareness breathed new life into its purpose.

Bisi became a beacon for Sankofa Foundation, as she took a more inclusive and empathetic approach to her leadership. But more importantly, she learned that a leader's strength not only lies in action but also in reflection. She established regular forums for open communication within Sankofa and encouraged the staff to voice their concerns and ideas.

Actions Bisi took to address self awareness
- Building Bridges. One of the first steps she took was to rebuild the bridges that had been burned. Bisi started by acknowledging her past mistakes and apologising to those she had unintentionally harmed. She then worked closely with her team to ensure that Sankofa's

goals were aligned with the needs and aspirations of the community.
- Renewed Partnerships. Bisi knew that for Sankofa to thrive, she needed to re-establish trust with not just her community but also with other stakeholders. She engaged in transparent discussions with donors, partners, and local government officials. Her newfound humility and genuine commitment to change rekindled relationships and opened avenues for new partnerships.
- The Heart of Sankofa. Under Bisi's transformed leadership, the Sankofa Foundation flourished. The women and children who were part of Sankofa's programs began to experience a more nurturing and empowering environment. This was mirrored in the community as the foundation's influence began to spread.

Years later, as Bisi prepared to pass the torch to a new leader, she reflected on her journey. The accolades and success were gratifying, but what truly resonated within her was the transformation she had undergone, which had been the catalyst for real change.

Suggestions of Building Blocks of Self-Awareness

Self-awareness is a crucial quality for successful social entrepreneurs. It helps you understand your strengths, weaknesses, emotions, and the effect you have on those around you. Here are some strategies to improve self-awareness:

- ❖ Practice Mindfulness. Mindfulness is the act of focusing on your present state and being conscious of your thoughts and feelings. This practice can help you understand your emotions and responses better, increasing self-awareness.
- ❖ Seek Feedback. Regularly seeking feedback from colleagues, team members, and mentors can provide insights into how others perceive you. Be open to this feedback and use it to inform your self-improvement efforts.

- ❖ Reflection and Journaling. Take time each day to reflect on your actions, decisions, and emotional states. Journaling about your thoughts and experiences can help you notice patterns and identify areas you need to work on.
- ❖ Emotional Intelligence Training. Improving your emotional intelligence can enhance your understanding of your own emotions and how you interact with others. There are many books, online resources, and courses that can help you in this area.
- ❖ Personality and Strengths Assessments. Tools like the Myers-Briggs Type Indicator or StrengthsFinder can provide insights into your personality traits and strengths. Understanding these can help you leverage your natural tendencies in your work as a social entrepreneur.
- ❖ Hire a Coach or Therapist. A professional coach or therapist can provide a safe space to explore your self-perception and behaviours.

They can provide unbiased feedback and strategies to enhance your self-awareness.
- ❖ Practise Active Listening. When you truly listen to others, you not only understand them better, but you also learn about your own biases and preconceptions.
- ❖ Engage in New Experiences. Pushing yourself out of your comfort zone by trying new things or meeting new people can be a great way to learn more about yourself. You might discover new passions or talents, or you might learn how you react under stress or unfamiliar circumstances.

Lack of Self Awareness Reflection Questions

1. What are some situations where I felt I lacked self-awareness? What triggered those situations?
2. Can I recall instances where my lack of self-awareness may have negatively impacted the communities or individuals my venture serves?

3. How does my lack of self-awareness affect my decision-making process?
4. In what ways have I noticed my emotions taking control of my actions before I fully understand them?
5. Have there been times when my emotions dictated decisions related to my venture, before I fully grasped the implications?
6. How often do I reflect on my actions, especially regarding their impact on my social mission and the communities I serve?
7. Do I find it challenging to accept feedback from community stakeholders or beneficiaries? What barriers might be causing this resistance?
8. How does my behaviour or decision-making change under funding pressures or logistical challenges? Am I conscious of these shifts when they happen?
9. Have I observed any recurring challenges or blind spots in how I approach my social venture, which I hadn't acknowledged before?

10. How often do I introspect about the genuine motives behind my entrepreneurial decisions? Are they impulsively driven by market dynamics or rooted in social impact?
11. What aspects of my past experiences, upbringing, or cultural background shape my approach towards social entrepreneurship?
12. How frequently am I taken aback by the reactions of community members, partners, or beneficiaries to my decisions or actions?

Chapter 3

LONE RANGER SYNDROME

The Costs of Independence Overdrive

This chapter unravels the journey of Amara, a social enterprise leader who, driven by her relentless passion and determination, unwittingly succumbs to the Lone Ranger syndrome.

Amara, a spirited and visionary young woman from Cameroon, embarked on a mission to empower marginalised women in her community. With unwavering dedication, she founded "Umoja Empowerment," a social enterprise aimed at providing vocational training, employment opportunities, and support to women striving for economic independence.

As Umoja Empowerment gained momentum, Amara, fueled by her passion and the weight of her responsibilities, assumed the role of the Lone Ranger. Driven by the belief that she alone could save the world, she shouldered every burden, from decision-making to project implementation, without seeking support from her team or the wider community.

Amara's lone pursuit of impact led her to become an overbearing and micro-managing leader. She believed that her vision and expertise were superior to anyone else's, stifling the creativity and potential of her team members. Her need for control overshadowed the collective wisdom and diverse perspectives that could have propelled Umoja Empowerment to greater heights.

As time passed, the strain of Amara's Lone Ranger syndrome began to erode the foundation of Umoja Empowerment. Team members felt disempowered and undervalued, causing discontent and high turnover. The disconnection between Amara's intentions and the realities faced by the women they served grew wider, jeopardising the enterprise's effectiveness.

One pivotal moment arrived when Amara attended a regional social entrepreneurship conference. She was humbled by the stories of other successful social enterprise leaders who attributed their achievements to collaboration, partnership, and shared leadership. Amara realised that she had been limiting the true potential of Umoja Empowerment by shouldering the burden alone.

A Shift in Paradigm
Determined to course-correct, Amara embarked on a transformative journey of self-reflection. She recognized the power of collaborative leadership and the importance of nurturing a culture of trust, empowerment, and shared ownership within her organisation.

Amara actively sought out partnerships and collaborations with like-minded organisations, experts, and community leaders. She invited her team to contribute their ideas and skills, empowering them to take ownership of their work and make meaningful contributions to the organisation's vision.

As Amara embraced collaborative leadership, the dynamics within Umoja Empowerment transformed. The team became more engaged, motivated, and innovative. With diverse voices at the table, the organisation was better equipped to address complex challenges and tap into new opportunities. Umoja Empowerment's impact began to flourish as collaborative efforts attracted more resources, expertise, and support. The women they served felt a deeper sense of empowerment, knowing that their voices were heard and their ideas valued.

Amara's shift from the Lone Ranger mindset redefined her leadership legacy. Umoja Empowerment became a shining example of the power of collaboration, inspiring other social entrepreneurs to seek partnerships and embrace collective leadership in their own endeavours.

Amara's journey serves as a poignant reminder that social entrepreneurship thrives when leaders embrace collaboration, foster a culture of shared ownership, and leverage the power of collective wisdom. The African proverb, "It takes a village to raise a child," resonates deeply in the realm of social entrepreneurship. Leaders like Amara, who recognize the limitations of the Lone Ranger syndrome, have the potential to unleash the transformative power of collaboration and drive sustainable change in their communities.

As social entrepreneurs, let us remember that we are not solitary warriors, but part of a larger ecosystem working towards a common goal. By embracing the spirit of collaboration, we can amplify our impact, tap into the collective wisdom of diverse perspectives, and build bridges that lead to a more equitable and inclusive future for all. Together, we can rewrite the narrative of social entrepreneurship, transforming it into a story of unity, resilience, and collective progress.

Amara's transformation from a Lone Ranger to a collaborative leader became an inspiration to many. In the wake of Amara's journey, collaborative networks and alliances began to emerge. Social entrepreneurs from diverse backgrounds joined forces to address complex challenges and create greater impact. These initiatives fostered knowledge sharing, resource pooling, and joint advocacy efforts, amplifying the collective voice of social entrepreneurship in Africa.

Amara's legacy extended beyond her own organisation. She dedicated herself to nurturing an ecosystem of collaboration, mentoring other social entrepreneurs, and supporting the growth of collaborative networks. She knew that by fostering a culture of collective action, they could create a movement that would outlive any individual venture.

Strategies for overcoming lone ranger syndrome
- ❖ Build a Trusted Team. Partner with individuals whose skills and values align with your vision. Trusting your team is essential to letting go of tasks that can be delegated.
- ❖ Delegate Strategically. Understand your strengths and weaknesses. Delegate tasks that are not your strengths to those better equipped to handle them.
- ❖ Mentorship and Peer Groups. Connect with mentors or join entrepreneur groups. Sharing experiences and challenges with peers can provide insights into the value of collaboration and teamwork.
- ❖ Seek External Feedback. Sometimes, an outsider's view can shed light on areas where collaboration could be beneficial. Don't be afraid to ask others about how they perceive you.

- ❖ Celebrate Team Achievements. Recognizing and celebrating collective achievements reinforces the value of teamwork and reduces the propensity to go it alone.
- ❖ Revisit Your Vision and Mission. Regularly remind yourself of your enterprise's larger purpose. Recognizing that the mission is bigger than any one individual can encourage collaboration and teamwork.

Lone Ranger Syndrome Self Reflection Questions

1. Reflecting on my entrepreneurial journey, which successes were amplified due to partnerships or teamwork?
2. What tangible positive impacts have I observed in my venture when I've entrusted tasks or responsibilities to my team or partners?
3. Who are the key collaborators or allies that have enhanced the potency and reach of my social initiatives?

4. How have past joint efforts or partnerships expanded the reach, scalability, or social impact of my venture?
5. What reservations or feelings arise when I contemplate seeking advice or collaboration in my social enterprise?
6. Have there been moments when I declined support to show that I can do it on my own? Did I later feel that it hindered my social mission?
7. Do I habitually take on more tasks than I can handle in my venture? What drives me to stretch myself thin?
8. When a solitary endeavour within my venture doesn't go as planned, how do I typically respond?
9. Why do I feel the urge to manage all facets of my social enterprise alone? Is it tied to fears about external perceptions, a need to validate my capabilities or anything else?
10. Am I prepared to recognise that seeking collaborations or partnerships doesn't

undermine my capability but can instead strengthen my venture's impact?

Chapter 4

FOUNDER BIAS SYNDROME

Unveiling the Blindfold

In the vibrant world of social entrepreneurship, the path of the founder is often marked by passion, resolve, and a profound attachment to their mission. Occasionally, however, the founder's personal beliefs can cloud their perspective, leading to a condition called founder syndrome. This chapter unravels the tale of Ropafadzo, a visionary in social entrepreneurship, whose journey was derailed by this very affliction.

A native of Zimbabwe, Ropafadzo was passionately committed to remedying the educational disparities faced by marginalised children in her community. Her personal experiences and fervour for change led to the inception of "Bright Beginnings," a social enterprise dedicated to providing quality education and empowerment to disadvantaged children.

As the organisation flourished, Ropafadzo's passionate commitment began to skew her objectivity. Her personal beliefs silently steered the strategies and decision-making process of Bright Beginnings. Convinced her perspective was universally applicable, she unintentionally ignored the cultural diversity of the community she sought to serve.

With time, the founder syndrome led to an expanding rift between Bright Beginnings and its target community. The programs, though conceived with the best intentions, no longer met the changing needs, goals, and cultural subtleties of the children and their families. The organisation's impact became stifled, and its relevance started to decline.

The pivotal moment arrived when the Board of Directors, aware of the growing disconnect, decided that a change in leadership was necessary. With a heavy heart, they decided to part ways with Ropafadzo, the founder of Bright Beginnings. The decision was hard, but they were confident that it was a necessary step for the organisation's survival and growth.

The successor, an experienced social entrepreneur with deep respect for community inclusiveness, brought fresh perspectives to the table. They prioritised establishing community consultations and co-creation workshops and placed the opinions of community members at the core of decision-making. This shift allowed for a more inclusive and community-focused approach.

Transparent communication, coupled with a genuine commitment to change, became the cornerstone of their leadership. The organisation acknowledged past shortcomings, and under the new leadership, began to regain the community's trust and support.

As the organisation transitioned to a more inclusive and community-centred model, the impact was significant. The programs became more attuned to the needs of the children and the community, enhancing growth, empowerment, and cultural preservation. This transformation echoed throughout African social entrepreneurship, cultivating an environment of inclusivity and responsiveness.

The story of Ropafadzo serves as a potent reminder of the potential pitfalls of founder syndrome in social entrepreneurship. It teaches us that it's crucial to acknowledge our biases, actively engage with the communities we serve, and co-create solutions that respect and value their diverse perspectives and needs.

As social entrepreneurs, we should aim to nurture humility, open-mindedness, and a deep regard for the wisdom and autonomy of the communities we strive to empower. By confronting and overcoming founder syndrome, we can create a more inclusive and efficient social entrepreneurship ecosystem that truly uplifts and transforms lives.

The Board's decision to remove Ropafadzo was met with mixed feelings, both within Bright Beginnings and the wider community. Some questioned whether the organisation would lose its guiding light, while others saw it as a necessary evolution. The challenge lay in steering the organisation through this transition without losing sight of its mission.

The new leader, chosen for their demonstrated commitment to community engagement and adaptability, knew they had big shoes to fill. Yet, they also understood the crucial need for a shift from the singular vision of a founder to a more collaborative and community-centred approach.

Under the new leadership, there was an immediate emphasis on listening. The voices that had felt sidelined were given a platform, and the organisation began to learn the rich diversity of dreams, aspirations, and needs that had been overlooked. For the first time in years, many in the community felt that Bright Beginnings was truly living up to its name.

The organisation's transformation became a beacon for others navigating similar challenges. It taught them that respecting and acknowledging the community's voice was not just a moral imperative but also a key to creating effective and sustainable solutions.

The decision to part ways with Ropafadzo was undoubtedly painful, but it served as a catalyst for much-needed change. As the organisation's influence began to expand, the Board of Directors could not help but feel a sense of validation. The hard decision had led to a more robust, inclusive, and impactful organisation.

Key Takeaways

Founder syndrome can have particular implications for social entrepreneurs embarking on a leadership journey.

1. Recognize and acknowledge your biases. Regularly check in with yourself about whether you're holding onto certain beliefs or ideas simply because they're yours.
2. As a social entrepreneur, you're driven by a mission. However, it's essential to differentiate between the core mission (the impact you want to make) and the methods (how you achieve that impact). While the task may remain constant, methods may need to change based on circumstances, evidence, or feedback.
3. Cultivate a culture where feedback is welcomed, from team members, beneficiaries, stakeholders, and other relevant parties.
4. Surround Yourself with Diverse Thinkers. Diverse teams lead to diverse viewpoints.

Having people who can challenge you and offer alternative perspectives is always healthy.

5. Stay Open to Pivot. Many successful ventures, both for-profit and social, have pivoted from their original idea. A willingness to change direction when necessary is crucial.
6. Balance Confidence with Humility. It's essential to have confidence in your vision, but it should be tempered with humility. Recognize that you don't have all the answers and be willing to learn and adapt.
7. Periodically step back and critically evaluate the venture's direction. Reflect on whether the decisions made still align with the intended social impact or if biases are clouding judgments.
8. Seek External Counsel. Mentors, advisors, or other experts in your field can provide invaluable outside perspectives. They can offer insights without being emotionally attached to the venture, helping to point out potential biases.

9. Be Prepared for Emotional Attachment. As a social entrepreneur, your venture might be deeply personal. Recognize that this emotional attachment can intensify founder bias. Being aware of this heightened emotional stake can help you navigate it more effectively.

Founder Syndrome Self Reflection Questions

1. As the founder of this organisation, how have I leveraged my passion and insight to steer the company, while also ensuring a space for collaborative decision-making and diverse insights?
2. When I receive feedback or face criticism, do I view it as an asset, a chance to improve and adapt, or do I sometimes allow my foundational beliefs to overshadow differing opinions?
3. In laying down the legacy of leadership, have I ensured a blueprint for succession that is both rooted in the organisation's origins and adaptive to its future needs?

4. Reflecting on my leadership, have I achieved a balance between upholding the organisation's initial vision and granting autonomy to other emerging leaders?
5. Beyond mere representation, how have I championed and facilitated true diversity and inclusion at decision-making tables within the organisation?
6. As the founder, have I instilled an organisational resilience that can thrive beyond my active involvement, ensuring the organisation's identity isn't solely anchored to me?
7. Recognizing the potential pitfalls of founder syndrome, what proactive steps have I taken, or can I take, to self-check and reduce its influence?
8. What further initiatives can I introduce to nurture an organisational culture that values transparency, embraces openness, and champions shared leadership?

Chapter 5

MESSIAH COMPLEX SYNDROME

Beyond the Hero Narrative

Ahmed, a proud son of Ghana, burned with a fervent desire to elevate his people. With this intention, he founded "EmpowerAfrica," aiming to counteract the challenges of his community through sustainable agriculture.

While Ahmed's early intentions were noble, the rapid success of EmpowerAfrica fostered a burgeoning Messiah Complex within him. Ahmed began to perceive himself as the exclusive solution to the community's multifaceted problems, overshadowing the communal wisdom and potential he once cherished. His belief in his unique ability to bring solutions eclipsed the insights and strengths of the very people he aimed to serve.

Ahmed's increasing insistence on his solutions, combined with his unintentional marginalisation of community voices, started hampering EmpowerAfrica's growth and efficiency. His overpowering leadership style suppressed innovation, making it increasingly difficult for the organisation to adapt and evolve effectively.

During a transformative social entrepreneurship summit, Ahmed encountered an eloquent elder who spoke of the profound change possible through collective action and community-led initiatives. While this was a golden opportunity for reflection and recalibration, Ahmed's entrenched Messiah Complex clouded his judgement. Rather than adopting this inclusive ethos, he persisted on his solitary mission, further distancing himself from the collective wisdom of his community.

EmpowerAfrica, once a beacon of hope, began to wane under Ahmed's monopolistic leadership. The very community and team Ahmed had hoped to uplift felt marginalised, leading to a pervasive sense of distrust and disengagement.

It was a series of such missteps, driven by his unchecked Messiah Complex, that contributed to the unfortunate decline of EmpowerAfrica. However, recognizing the errors in his approach, Ahmed earnestly sought mentorship and feedback. Through introspection and learning, he worked towards mending the bridges he had unintentionally burnt, striving to restore EmpowerAfrica's original mission and the trust of his community.

Lessons from the Messiah Complex
- ❖ Humility in Leadership. It's vital for leaders to remain humble and recognize that success is a collective effort.
- ❖ Listen Actively. Always remain receptive to feedback from the community and stakeholders. They are often best positioned to provide insights and understand their needs.

- Beware of Ego. Success can sometimes inflate one's self-perception. Regular self-reflection and humility are necessary to ensure that ego doesn't overshadow the enterprise's mission.
- Valuing Diverse Perspectives. A leader should not only be open to different viewpoints but actively seek them to make well-rounded decisions.
- Sustainable Ambition. While ambition is laudable, it must be tempered with pragmatism to ensure the organisation's actions are sustainable.
- Recognizing the Limits of One's Role. A leader is an essential part of an organisation, but not the sole determinant of its fate.
- Nurturing a Culture of Shared Ownership. Encouraging a sense of ownership among all team members ensures that the organisation's success is a shared journey.

Messiah Syndrome Self Reflection Questions

1. As I navigate my entrepreneurial journey, how frequently do I actively seek and celebrate the existing assets, talents, and successes within the community? How can I better co-create with them, building upon these assets to co-envision and actualize sustainable solutions?

2. While I'm driven to make a difference, can I discern instances when my initiatives might have bypassed or undervalued the inherent strengths and systems of the community?

3. When I receive insights or feedback, especially from community members, how do I reconcile their experiential wisdom with my entrepreneurial knowledge? Do I give their perspectives the weight they deserve in shaping our shared journey?

4. Are there moments when my vision might have inadvertently dimmed the innovative ideas of my team or partners? How can I more

effectively tap into the collective brilliance within our mission-driven

5. How am I fostering an environment where everyone feels they're a valued co-creator, rather than merely supporting actors in a singular hero narrative?

6. What proactive measures can I undertake to keep any latent Messiah tendencies in check, and to bolster collaborative agency and joint solution-building?

7. Can I reflect on times when fueled by a rush to "rescue" or "fix", my interventions might've rippled into unforeseen circumstances?

8. How do I ensure my fervour to enact change doesn't inadvertently overshadow the intrinsic strengths, traditions, and resilience of the communities I engage with?

Chapter 6

SUPERHERO SYNDROME

Invincibility Illusion: strength in vulnerability

In the sprawling plains of Uganda, there was a charismatic social enterprise leader named Mirembe Madaki. A native of the region, Mirembe's early life was marked by hardship. His vision to overcome his own adversities led to the founding of a social enterprise called Tusaidiane, which means "let's help each other" in Swahili. Tusaidiane aimed to create sustainable livelihoods for communities through agricultural innovations, empowering them to fight poverty, and supporting education.

Mirembe was revered as the epitome of resilience and innovation. His vision was pure, and his words spoke to the hearts of many, mobilising communities and international investors alike. The media catapulted him to fame, hailing him as the modern-day African superhero. His image graced international platforms and accolades began to roll in.

However, as Tusaidiane grew, so did the expectations on Mirembe's shoulders. The vibrant leader began to exhibit the signs of what is known as the Superhero Syndrome. Superhero Syndrome is a term used to describe the tendency of leaders to believe they are invincible and must personally handle all issues. Instead of delegating tasks and building a team, Mirembe started to take on more responsibilities and made decisions unilaterally.

His close colleagues, such as Amina, the Head of Community Outreach and Ahmed the Financial Manager, tried to reason with him. However, Mirembe, caught in his belief that he alone could steer the ship through troubled waters, disregarded their advice.

As Mirembe tried to control every aspect of Tusaidiane, the organisation's initial success began to waver. Projects started to falter due to his lack of attention to detail, as he was spread too thin. The communities who were initially mobilised and energised, began to feel distanced as Mirembe was no longer as accessible. The media, who had once been his strongest ally, began to question his management style.

Amina and Ahmed , along with other team members, held an intervention. They hoped to remind Mirembe of Tusaidiane's original values of collaboration and shared decision-making. They presented testimonials from community members, and data showing the decline in the effectiveness of the organisation.

For a brief moment, Mirembe's eyes welled up with tears. He seemed to recognize the destruction his Superhero Syndrome had caused. However, his ego, now grown massive, took over. He lashed out, accusing his team of betrayal. Over the next year,

Tusaidiane spiralled downwards. Key team members left, and funders withdrew their support. The communities, feeling abandoned, sought alternatives to the now hollow promises of Tusaidiane. Mirembe Madaki, the once celebrated African social enterprise leader, had become a cautionary tale.

In the aftermath of Tusaidiane's downfall, the once-flourishing organisation became a shadow of its former self. The communities, which had put their faith in the enterprise, were left disillusioned.

However, among the rubble, a glimmer of hope remained. Amina and Ahmed , who had been integral members of Tusaidiane since its inception, couldn't let go of their love for the mission that had initially driven the organisation. They reached out to other former colleagues, and slowly but surely, a core group started forming. They named this new incarnation of the organisation "Tumaini", which means hope in Swahili.

Tumaini started small, focusing on listening to the communities and involving them in decision-making processes. Unlike Mirembe, Amina, who took up the role of the leader, made it clear that leadership was to be shared and based on trust and collaboration. They introduced mentorship programs and a rotational leadership system to ensure that no single person would carry the weight of the whole organisation.

Meanwhile, Mirembe had receded into obscurity. His dreams shattered, and his name tarnished, he wandered aimlessly. He embarked on a personal journey across different regions of Africa. He observed the simple lives of the people, their community spirit, and their undying hope.

One day, while in a small village in Tanzania, Mirembe witnessed a community group successfully running a cooperative that closely resembled his initial vision for Tusaidiane. The joy and sense of purpose he saw in the community members struck him profoundly.

Something inside Mirembe shifted. It was a moment of awakening. The superhero facade crumbled, revealing a humbled man who finally acknowledged his fallibility.

Mirembe returned to his homeland. He reached out to Amina and Ahmed, not to reclaim his former position but to apologise and offer his support in any way he could. The reunion was emotional; a blend of bitterness, forgiveness, and a rekindling of a shared vision.

Lessons from the Messiah Complex

- ❖ Shared Leadership is Crucial. No one person holds all the answers. For sustainable impact, social entrepreneurs should actively promote shared leadership and collaborative decision-making.
- ❖ Stay Grounded. While passion drives social initiatives, humility ensures they remain effective. Recognize the efforts of everyone

involved and celebrate collective achievements.

- ❖ Avoid Saviour Mentality. Recognize that impactful change is a collective effort. The role of a social entrepreneur is to facilitate and empower, not to "rescue" or "save."
- ❖ Foster an Inclusive Culture. Encourage a culture of inclusivity and collaboration within your organisation. This ensures diverse perspectives are considered and avoids the pitfalls of a centralised decision-making process.
- ❖ Acknowledge Limits. Every leader has strengths and limitations. By recognizing one's boundaries, a social entrepreneur can better leverage partnerships and collaborations to fill gaps.
- ❖ Balance Passion with Pragmatism. While it's essential to be driven by passion, it's equally crucial to approach challenges with a pragmatic mindset. This ensures that ambitions align with reality.

❖ **Celebrate Collective Impact.** Recognize and champion the successes and contributions of the broader team and community. Shared accomplishments amplify impact and foster deeper engagements.

Superhero Syndrome Self Reflection Questions

1. How consistently do I recognize and amplify the innate capabilities, insights, and solutions within both the community I serve and my team, instead of trying to address every challenge personally?

2. How frequently do I find myself stepping in to tackle challenges alone? Can I pinpoint moments when this lone approach may have inadvertently led to fatigue or missed opportunities for innovation?

3. Am I truly capitalising on the diverse strengths and skills within my team, or do I tend to absorb roles and tasks that could be more efficiently executed by others?

4. How often do I feel the need to project an unyielding front to my team or stakeholders? How might this perception of invulnerability impact my willingness to seek assistance, or acknowledge areas of uncertainty?
5. Can I reflect on instances where my inclination to 'save the day' might have inadvertently stifled the growth, initiative, or creativity of team members or partners?
6. How am I nurturing an environment where each member feels confident to voice ideas and share expertise, and where iterative learning is embraced as a pathway to refinement and growth?
7. How do I process and pivot from challenges or failures? Am I imposing undue expectations on myself to always be the unerring protagonist in our mission's narrative?
8. How am I acknowledging and addressing my own needs for rest, rejuvenation, and reflection, understanding that enduring impact stems from sustainable practices?

9. What proactive steps can I initiate to evolve from a 'solo superhero' mentality to a more collaborative, inclusive, and resilient leadership model?

Chapter 7

COMPASSION FATIGUE

A Vision Derailed by the Weight of Compassion

Darweshi Nkechi was a woman whose spirit soared as high as Kilimanjaro. Born in a small village in Tanzania, she was the epitome of resilience and determination. She fought tooth and nail to attain an education, overcoming obstacles that most people could not fathom. In her early thirties, Darweshi founded Sauti ya Jamii (Voice of the Community), a social enterprise aimed at uplifting marginalised communities in East Africa.

Darweshi's enterprise rapidly gained traction. She created community-driven agriculture programs, helped build schools, and initiated women empowerment projects. Sauti ya Jamii became a beacon of hope for the people and a testament to Darweshi's unyielding spirit.

However, as the enterprise grew, so did the burdens on Darweshi's shoulders. She had become not just a leader, but the heart of the communities she served. Everyone looked up to her; her presence was a constant source of inspiration and solace.

The stories she encountered daily were heart-wrenching. The tears of a widowed mother unable to feed her children, the frail hands of the aged longing for medical care, and the dimmed sparkle in the eyes of children with no schools to attend – all tugged at Darweshi's heartstrings.

The outside world often only saw the success of Sauti ya Jamii; they didn't see the exhaustion enveloping Darweshi's soul. She worked relentlessly, sometimes forgetting to eat or sleep, driven by her compassion for the people she served.

As the years passed, the burden of her relentless compassion began to take its toll. Darweshi developed what is known as 'compassion fatigue'.

This is a condition common among caregivers and social workers, where constant exposure to the suffering of others leads to emotional and physical exhaustion. It's often characterised by a decrease in empathy, increased cynicism, and a diminished sense of personal accomplishment.

Darweshi's once vibrant spirit began to wane. She started distancing herself from the stories that once moved her to act. She grew impatient, irritable, and less engaging with the community members.

The decline in Darweshi's well-being was reflected in the waning effectiveness of Sauti ya Jamii. Decision-making became haphazard, funding was misallocated, and the trust she had built within the communities started to erode.

She began to realise that her compassion fatigue was undermining everything she had built. It took an intervention from a close friend and mentor, Dr.

Benjamin Okeke, for her to recognize the necessity of self-care in leadership.

Dr. Okeke, a renowned psychologist and supporter of Sauti ya Jamii, helped Darweshi understand that compassion is a finite resource if not nurtured. He emphasised the importance of delegating responsibilities, establishing emotional boundaries, and taking time for self-renewal.

With this newfound insight, Darweshi embarked on a sabbatical, passing the leadership of Sauti ya Jamii to her capable team. She delved into meditation, therapy, and connected with her roots.

Several months later, Darweshi returned to Sauti ya Jamii, not as its sole heart but as part of a greater heart that beats for the welfare of the communities. She implemented a structure that promoted collective leadership and emotional well-being among the staff.

Though the journey of Sauti ya Jamii encountered a storm, Darweshi's story serves as a reminder to social entrepreneurs that they, too, are human. Her life is a testament that sometimes, the most compassionate thing a leader can do is to recognize the importance of replenishing their own soul for the greater good.

As Darweshi integrated herself back into Sauti ya Jamii, she realised the importance of not only healing herself but also ensuring that her team was equipped to handle the emotional burdens of their work. She started by introducing wellness programs within the organisation. Darweshi invited mental health professionals to hold workshops, and she emphasised the importance of a balanced life to her team.

Furthermore, she started a mentorship program within Sauti ya Jamii, encouraging the senior members to provide guidance and support to the newer ones. This created a sense of community within the organisation itself, ensuring that the members could find solace and understanding amongst each other.

Externally, Darweshi also sought partnerships with other social enterprises and NGOs. By doing so, she was able to share resources, knowledge, and best practices. This not only bolstered Sauti ya Jamii's impact but also helped alleviate some of the pressure on Darweshi and her team, as they now had allies in their mission.

Perhaps one of the most transformative steps Darweshi took was establishing a community counsel within the areas Sauti ya Jamii served. This counsel comprised individuals from the local communities who could voice their concerns, share their stories, and participate actively in decision-making. This democratisation of voice not only empowered the communities but also diversified the emotional and operational load that was previously borne almost solely by Darweshi.

As the years went by, Sauti ya Jamii flourished again, this time more sustainably and more aligned with the well-being of both the communities it served and the individuals who served them.

As for Darweshi, she found a more profound sense of fulfilment. She had learned that true leadership does not mean carrying the weight of the world alone but creating a network of support and compassion that uplifts everyone involved. She became an advocate for mental health and self-care among social entrepreneurs and leaders. Darweshi's journey of overcoming compassion fatigue evolved into a powerful message, which she took to conferences, schools, and communities.

Years later, Darweshi Nkechi was recognized with numerous accolades for her contributions to social entrepreneurship and her commitment to community development.

In her acceptance speech for the prestigious African Leadership Impact Award, she said, "Our spirits are like wells; they can quench the thirst of many. But if we do not take care to replenish them, they may run dry. To serve others, we must not forget to serve ourselves."

Darweshi's story became an inspiration and a cautionary tale for emerging leaders. Through her trials and eventual triumphs, she showed that in the pursuit of a better world, the guardians of compassion must also guard their own hearts and well-being.

Lessons from Compassion Fatigue
1. Importance of Self-care. For leaders immersed in emotionally intense work, self-care is not a luxury but a necessity for sustaining their mission.
2. Setting Boundaries. Establishing clear boundaries between personal life and work is essential to maintain emotional balance.

3. Self-care Isn't Selfish. Taking time for self-renewal isn't a luxury but a necessity. This can be in the form of rest, hobbies, therapy, or other rejuvenating activities.
4. Seek Peer Support. Engaging with peers can offer validation and understanding, helping to process and manage the emotional toll of the work.
5. Diversify Responsibilities. Avoid concentrating emotionally taxing roles or tasks on one individual. Distribute responsibilities to ensure no single person is overwhelmed.
6. Building a Supportive Environment. An NGO should cultivate an environment that encourages emotional support among team members.
7. Sustainable Empathy. Learn to balance empathy with emotional sustainability to ensure long-term effectiveness.

Compassion Fatigue Self Reflection Questions

1. What competencies and emotional intelligence skills have I developed as a social entrepreneur that assist me in navigating the emotional demands I am encountering?
2. How regularly do I reach out to my community of fellow social entrepreneurs, mentors, or close ones when I feel drained?
3. Amid the inherent challenges of social entrepreneurship, can I recount the victories, transformations, or testimonials that rekindle my passion and purpose?
4. How do I tap into my previous encounters with adversity to fortify my resolve when confronting compassion fatigue in my current journey?
5. Have I sensed any diminishing intensity in my compassion or connection with the communities and causes I serve? What are its tangible indications?
6. How do I strike a balance in absorbing the emotional weight of my mission while also

ensuring my own well-being? Have I integrated consistent self-care rituals?

7. How frequently do I grant myself the liberty to disconnect, rejuvenate, and realign with my mission's core intent?

8. How adept am I at delineating limits to safeguard my emotional health amidst the often intense demands of social entrepreneurship?

9. How have I structured my work-life demarcation? Is there a continuous preoccupation with my initiative even during designated downtime?

10. How often do I confide in or consult peers about the emotional intricacies of my social enterprise? Have I cultivated a nurturing circle for mutual support and mentorship?

11. Have I discerned manifestations like emotional distancing, fatigue, or increased scepticism in my entrepreneurial journey? What strategies can be employed to counter these?

12. How might I refine my strategic approach to my venture's activities, ensuring a more sustainable, compassionate involvement that minimises compassion fatigue?

13. Given my unique entrepreneurial journey and the signs I've observed, what personalised measures can I implement to tackle compassion fatigue, ensuring I remain both effective and emotionally aligned with my mission?

Chapter 8

PERFECTIONIST SYNDROME

In the Shadow of the Ideal

Mamadou Adom, with his infectious smile and fervent intellect, was a man on a mission. Born in Accra, Ghana, he had been a prodigy since his youth. His perfectionist tendencies helped him achieve the highest accolades in education, but they would later prove to be both a blessing and a curse.

Mamadou's vision was unambiguous; he aimed to eradicate energy poverty in rural areas of Ghana through solar technology. This led to the genesis of Takoradi, a social enterprise that sought to bring renewable energy solutions to the remotest corners of the country.

In the beginning, Mamadou's perfectionism seemed to be an asset. His attention to detail, insistence on the highest quality, and his relentless pursuit of excellence propelled Takoradi into the limelight. Investors and partners were drawn to the enterprise's impeccably presented plans and Mamadou's unwavering commitment to his cause.

However, as Takoradi began to implement projects, the cracks started to show. Mamadou's perfectionism evolved into an unrelenting force that stifled progress. His obsession with ensuring that every detail matched his ideal vision often led to indefinite delays.

As the team sought to install solar panels in villages, Mamadou's insistence on using only a particular type of solar cell, which was not easily available, caused months of delay. Moreover, his proclivity to micromanage every aspect of the projects rendered his team feeling disempowered and dejected.

Mamadou's vision of perfection also strained relationships with partners. When presented with collaborative proposals, he would often decline or spend weeks scrutinising every detail. This led to missed opportunities and a growing frustration among his allies.

What was most striking was the toll Mamadou's perfectionism took on the very people he aimed to serve. Villages awaiting electricity continued to languish in darkness. Children couldn't study at night, and healthcare facilities struggled without adequate power. The quest for perfection was, in essence, depriving the community of progress.

It was during an annual review meeting that Mamadou was confronted by Naa Ashorkor, a project manager within Takoradi, who had seen the impact of the delays firsthand. She shared stories of the villages - stories of dreams wilting in the shadows. Tears streaming down her face, she implored

Mamadou to see that sometimes good and timely can make more difference than perfect and delayed.

This raw confrontation served as a wake-up call for Mamadou . He realised that his perfectionist tendencies, while rooted in good intentions, were derailing the very mission he had set out to achieve.

Determined to change course, Mamadou sought counselling and began reading about adaptive leadership styles. He started to appreciate the concept of 'progress over perfection'.

One of the first changes Mamadou made was to empower his team. He stepped back from micromanagement and encouraged team members to take ownership of projects. He also started accepting that there are different paths to achieving the end goal and that his vision of perfection was not the only way.

Additionally, Mamadou adopted a more collaborative approach to partnerships. He began to trust and rely on the expertise of others, understanding that synergy could often achieve more than solitary perfection. Over time, Takoradi regained momentum. Solar panels were installed in villages, lighting up the lives of thousands. The enterprise, once stifled by the chains of perfectionism, began to breathe and grow with newfound freedom.

Mamadou's transformation was encapsulated when a young entrepreneur asked him for advice at a conference. He smiled warmly and said, "Strive for excellence, but do not let the mirage of perfection paralyse you. Progress, even in small steps, lights the path for change." Mamadou Adom's journey through the labyrinth of perfectionism became a lesson for leaders in social enterprises and beyond. It reminded them of the delicate balance between the pursuit of excellence and the agility required to make a tangible impact.

Takoradi, under Mamadou's adaptive leadership, burgeoned into a pan-African beacon of renewable energy solutions. It was no longer just about the perfection of technology; it became a testament to the perfecting of the human spirit, understanding, and adaptability.

As Mamadou moved forward, he cultivated an environment of open communication within Takoradi. He encouraged feedback from his team and the communities they served. This feedback became an invaluable resource for the organisation to grow and adapt to the ever-changing landscapes and challenges they faced.

Years later, during the inauguration of a solar-powered hospital in a rural area, Mamadou stood among the crowd as they celebrated. The joy and gratitude in their eyes, the laughter of children who would now have better opportunities, and the relief of the medical staff who could now serve more efficiently – all these painted the true picture of success.

Mamadou realised that in seeking an unattainable perfection, he had almost missed the essence of his work, which was to bring light and hope. His evolution from a stringent perfectionist to an adaptive leader was a transformation that did not just change his life but the lives of countless others.

Overcoming Perfectionist syndrome
1. Embrace Imperfection. Perfectionism can be paralysing and inhibit innovation and creativity. Learning to embrace imperfection can unlock new opportunities and foster a culture of continuous learning and improvement in your social
2. Learn to Delegate. No one can do everything perfectly. Trusting your team and delegating tasks effectively can lead to more efficient operations and help prevent burnout.

3. Balance is Key. Maintaining a balanced perspective is essential. Strive for excellence but understand that perfection is unattainable and unnecessary. Prioritise tasks and focus on what really matters.
4. Failure is Part of the Process. Perfectionism often stems from a fear of failure. However, failure is an integral part of entrepreneurship and often provides valuable lessons. Adopt a growth mindset that views setbacks as opportunities for learning.
5. Manage Expectations. Set realistic expectations for yourself and your team. Unreasonable standards can lead to stress, demotivation, and decreased productivity.
6. Practice Self-Compassion. Be kind to yourself when things don't go perfectly. Acknowledging that everyone makes mistakes can alleviate the pressure of perfectionism.
7. Celebrate Progress. Instead of focusing solely on end results, celebrate progress and small

victories along the way. This can motivate your team and foster a positive work culture.

Perfectionist Syndrome Self Reflection Questions

1. In my initiatives, do I frequently find myself expending an undue amount of time refining projects beyond what's pragmatically impactful or what the community genuinely needs?
2. How does my aspiration for flawlessness guide the decisions I make in my venture, and does it enhance or hinder the scalability and efficacy of my impact?
3. What is the ripple effect of my perfectionistic tendencies on my team? Does it instil a culture of excellence, or does it inadvertently cultivate a tense and high-pressure environment?
4. Do I hesitate to delegate responsibilities, believing that only I can achieve the desired impeccable outcomes? How does this impact the growth and capacity of my team?

5. How frequently am I apprehensive about potential errors or external critiques? How does this sentiment shape the risks I'm willing to take or the innovations I pursue?

6. How do I emotionally and strategically navigate situations when outcomes deviate from my idealised vision? Does this trigger disproportionate stress or self-doubt?

7. Do I perpetually set towering, perhaps unattainable, benchmarks for myself, my team, or my venture? What drives this mentality?

8. How might I foster an appreciation for the value in 'adequacy', understanding that perfection might sometimes be the enemy of the 'good' in social entrepreneurship?

9. In my entrepreneurial journey, do I pause to acknowledge and revel in incremental achievements, or is my gaze rigidly fixed on the ultimate, flawless goal?

10. How can I nurture a more forgiving, understanding perspective towards setbacks, learning curves, and the inevitable

imperfections, ensuring a sustainable, empathetic leadership approach?

Chapter 9

BURN OUT SYNDROME

Running on empty: Extinguishing the flame

This chapter delves into the life of Sofia, a social entrepreneur from Equatorial Guinea who dedicated herself to combating hunger through her social enterprise, NourishWave. Her relentless commitment eventually gave way to burnout, undermining both her leadership and the enterprise she cherished.

Sofia, a nutritionist by profession, envisioned a world free from hunger and malnutrition. Her heart ached for the impoverished communities lacking access to nutritious food. With boundless passion and energy, she founded NourishWave, aimed at providing affordable and nutritious meals to underprivileged communities.

In its nascent stage, NourishWave became the epitome of innovation and social impact. Sofia was the driving force behind its success. She worked tirelessly, sometimes clocking 18 hours a day, networking, fundraising, managing operations, and community outreach.

As the months turned into years, Sofia's relentless pace began to take a toll on her. The signs were subtle at first; she was increasingly irritable, her concentration waned, and her once optimistic disposition grew clouded.

NourishWave's staff began to notice a change in Sofia's demeanour. The spirited leader who once infused hope and enthusiasm seemed constantly drained and dispirited.

Sofia's commitment to NourishWave consumed her. Her relationships suffered, her health declined, and her motivation waned. She felt as though she was walking through a perpetual fog, unable to find clarity of purpose.

The once-thriving NourishWave suffered in tandem with Sofia. The team felt directionless, initiatives faltered, and the enterprise's impact began to decline. During a community event, Sofia collapsed. She was rushed to the hospital, where the doctor confirmed that she was suffering from severe exhaustion and burnout. It was a wake-up call for Sofia, who realised that her way of leading was unsustainable and damaging both to herself and to NourishWave.

Sofia took a medical leave of absence and during this time, began a journey of self-reflection and recovery. She sought counselling, rekindled relationships, and reevaluated her priorities. She also realised that NourishWave needed a more sustainable leadership model. One that did not rely solely on her but instead distributed responsibilities and cultivated leadership within the organisation.

Upon her return, Sofia implemented significant changes in NourishWave. She delegated responsibilities, set realistic goals, and created a more collaborative and supportive work environment. She also encouraged work-life balance, not only for her team but for herself as well.

With Sofia's renewed approach, NourishWave regained its momentum. The team was invigorated, and the enterprise's social impact flourished.

Sofia also began to speak openly about her experience with burnout. She realised that her story could serve as both a cautionary tale and an inspiration for other social entrepreneurs. She started an initiative within NourishWave that focused on mental health and well-being for social entrepreneurs. Through workshops, resources, and forums, Sofia became an advocate for sustainable and compassionate leadership.

Sofia's journey is a poignant reminder that even the most passionate flames, if not tended to, can consume the vessel they burn within. Social entrepreneurs, in their noble quests, must recognize the importance of self-care and sustainability in leadership. NourishWave, under Sofia's reinvigorated leadership, continued to make strides in combating hunger, and it also became a beacon for how social enterprises can thrive sustainably.

Sofia's experience with burnout is not unique among social entrepreneurs. The drive to make a positive impact can sometimes be so overpowering that it clouds the necessity for balance and self-care. Through her renewal, Sofia demonstrated that true leadership is not just guiding an organisation but also knowing when to tend to one's own well-being.

In her later years, Sofia often reflected on the lessons learned from the flames of burnout. She became a mentor for aspiring social entrepreneurs and always emphasised the importance of pacing oneself, setting realistic goals, and fostering a culture of empathy and support. In her later years, Sofia often found solace in mentoring young social entrepreneurs. She felt that her experiences could provide the lantern for many who walk the path she once did. One of her protégés, a young woman from a country that NourishWave served, became the CEO of a budding social enterprise focused on women's health.

Sofia often said that the sparkle in the eyes of the young leaders she mentored was the most profound reward. It was a sign that the flames she once feared had found their purpose in igniting countless torches of change.

Suggestions on Overcoming Burnout
1. Understand the Signs. Recognize the early signs of burnout, such as chronic fatigue, irritability, disillusionment, reduced performance, and physical symptoms like headaches or stomach problems.
2. Set Realistic Expectations. While it's noble to want to change the world, understand that it

won't happen overnight. Celebrate small wins and set achievable goals.

3. Unplug. Digital detox periods, like staying away from screens, social media, and email, can help rejuvenate your mind.
4. Take a Vacation. Sometimes, you need an extended break to recharge. It might seem impossible, but your enterprise will benefit from a refreshed and rejuvenated you.
5. Join a Community. Connect with other social entrepreneurs. Sharing challenges, experiences, and solutions can provide both emotional and practical support.
6. Set Boundaries. Establish a clear separation between work and personal life. This might mean setting specific work hours, taking regular breaks, or fully disconnecting on days off.
7. Prioritise Self-Care. Regular exercise, a healthy diet, and adequate sleep can significantly affect your mood and energy levels. Engaging

in hobbies and activities you enjoy can also help recharge your batteries.
8. Practice Mindfulness. Mindfulness techniques, such as meditation or deep-breathing exercises, can reduce stress and increase feelings of well-being.
9. Seek Support. Don't hesitate to reach out to colleagues, friends, or mental health professionals if you're feeling overwhelmed. Having a strong support network can make a significant difference.
10. Delegate and Collaborate. Share responsibilities with your team or volunteers. Delegating not only lessens your workload but also builds capacity within your organisation.

Burnout Self Reflection Questions

1. Amidst the challenges of my social enterprise, which of my inherent strengths has consistently fortified me?

2. In moments when my passion for change was most palpable, what core attributes of mine were in play?
3. Contemplating my triumphs, which unique qualities and resources did I tap into to drive impact and overcome barriers?
4. Who has consistently championed my cause and stood by me? How might I deepen my connection with them to navigate current challenges?
5. Are there specific occurrences or stressors that have amplified my feelings of burnout or disengagement of late?
6. How regularly do I carve out time for rejuvenating activities and genuine self-care amidst the hustle of social change?
7. When did I last consciously disconnect from my venture to rest, rejuvenate, and refocus?
8. How would I assess my present physical vitality and zest?

9. Have there been significant shifts in my sleep rhythm, eating habits, or general well-being indicative of burnout?

Chapter 10

IMPOSTER SYNDROME

Hidden in Plain sight

This chapter unveils the journey of Akinyi Odhiambo, a social entrepreneur whose remarkable vision was nearly eclipsed by the shadows of impostor syndrome. Akinyi, born in a small village near Nairobi, Kenya, was a spirited and determined individual. The daughter of farmers, she grew up witnessing the toil of her community, the disparity between the rich and poor, and the untapped potential that lay within the lands and the people.

With a passion for sustainable agriculture and community empowerment, Akinyi established 'Harvest of Hope', a social enterprise that aimed to empower local farmers through sustainable practices and access to broader markets. In the initial years,

Harvest of Hope saw unprecedented success. Through innovative agricultural techniques and robust community engagement, the enterprise revolutionised farming in the region. Akinyi, the heart and soul of the venture, became a celebrated figure.

As Harvest of Hope's impact grew, so did the attention on Akinyi. She was invited to international conferences, was awarded grants, and became a symbol of change in the social enterprise space. Despite the accolades and success, Akinyi started to feel a growing unease within her. With each passing achievement, she felt like an actor on a stage, waiting for the audience to discover that she didn't belong. The whispers of doubt grew into voices as she constantly felt that she was not deserving or capable of leading this movement.

She saw herself as a simple farmer's daughter who had somehow tricked the world into believing she was more. She worried that someone else could have done it better. As the impostor syndrome gripped Akinyi, her decision-making and leadership began to falter. She avoided public speaking engagements, became indecisive, and distanced herself from the team. Harvest of Hope, which had been a beacon of innovation and community empowerment, began to lose its momentum.

Marjorie, a childhood friend and confidant of Akinyi, noticed the change. One evening, under the starlit African sky, Marjorie confronted Akinyi. Through tears, Akinyi shared her fears and doubts. Marjorie, in her wisdom, reminded Akinyi of the little girl who helped her father in the fields, the teenager who taught her friends to read, and the woman whose vision had transformed lives.

With the support of Marjorie and others, Akinyi sought counselling. She also started engaging with other social entrepreneurs and realised that impostor syndrome was a common phenomenon.

She embarked on a journey of self-acceptance, recognizing that her roots were not a limitation but the very foundation upon which her strength was built.

Rejuvenated and grounded, Akinyi returned to Harvest of Hope with a renewed spirit. She opened up about her struggles, and this vulnerability resonated with the team. They became more committed and cohesive. Under her leadership, Harvest of Hope expanded its reach and impact. However, this time, Akinyi's leadership was not driven by the validation of others, but by the conviction and authenticity of her purpose.

As years passed, Harvest of Hope became not just a social enterprise but a movement that transcended borders. Akinyi, through her trials and tribulations, had sown seeds deeper than the soil; seeds of honesty, humility, and resilience. She established the 'Seeds of Authenticity' initiative within Harvest of Hope, which aimed at nurturing personal development and mental health for social entrepreneurs and community leaders. She understood the importance of addressing the psychological hurdles that so often plague the minds of those who dare to change the world.

Akinyi dedicated a portion of her later years to mentorship. She engaged with young social entrepreneurs across Africa and shared her story with the world. Her talks on overcoming impostor syndrome became a source of inspiration for many.

One of the most impactful sessions was when Akinyi returned to her village to address the community and the next generation of leaders. She spoke not just of her successes but of her fears and doubts. She told them that every person, regardless of their background, would face moments when shadows of doubt cloud their path. But it is in embracing one's roots, one's truth, and one's humanity, that the path is illuminated.

Overcoming Imposter Syndrome

1. Acknowledge your feelings. The first step in dealing with imposter syndrome is acknowledging it. Recognize that it's a common experience, especially among high achievers and those trying to create social impact. Accepting that it's okay to have these feelings can be a huge relief.

2. Value your unique journey. As a social entrepreneur, your path is often non-traditional, which may lead to feelings of inadequacy when comparing yourself to others in more traditional roles. Remember that your unique journey, with all its ups and downs, contributes to your distinctive insights and abilities.

3. Celebrate your successes. Regularly reflect on and celebrate your accomplishments, no matter how small they may seem. This will help to reinforce the reality of your skills and competencies. Write down your achievements

and reflect on them when you're feeling like an imposter.

4. Embrace learning and growth. As a social entrepreneur, you're likely working in complex, constantly evolving environments. Understand that not knowing everything is not a sign of inadequacy but an opportunity for learning and growth.

5. Avoid Comparison. Everyone's journey is unique. Comparing your chapter two to someone else's chapter ten is not constructive. Remember, social media and public presentations usually highlight successes and omit the struggles and hard work.

6. Find a support network. Connect with other social entrepreneurs who understand the challenges you're facing. They can provide reassurance, share their own experiences, and offer valuable advice. Mentorship can also be an excellent source of support and learning.

7. Practise self-compassion. Be kind to yourself when you make mistakes or face setbacks.

Treat them as part of the journey rather than evidence of incompetence.

8. Reframe your thoughts. Challenge and reframe your critical inner voice with more positive, empowering narratives. If you find yourself thinking, "I'm not good enough," try to reframe that thought with, "I'm doing my best, and that's enough."

9. Seek professional help. If imposter syndrome is causing significant stress or anxiety, consider seeking help from a mental health professional. Cognitive-behavioural therapy, for instance, can provide strategies to change the negative thinking patterns associated with imposter syndrome.

10. Mindfulness and meditation. Practising mindfulness and meditation can help you stay focused on the present and reduce negative self-judgement. It allows you to observe your feelings of imposter syndrome without getting caught up in them.

Imposter Syndrome Self Reflection Questions

1. Reflecting on my journey as a social entrepreneur, what unique strengths and capabilities have I harnessed to make a difference?
2. Can I recount an instance where I faced major obstacles in my mission? What innate qualities or external resources empowered me to push past those hurdles?
3. Are there recurring scenarios or tasks that amplify my feelings of being an imposter within the social entrepreneurship sphere?
4. Deep down, what is my biggest apprehension when plagued by imposter feelings? Is it doubts about my legitimacy, dread of not living up to expectations, or something else?
5. How do I internalise accolades or recognition for my social ventures? Do I ascribe my accomplishments to serendipity or outside influences, or do I genuinely honour my dedication and expertise?

6. What self-talk emerges during moments of imposter syndrome? Are there recurring themes or sentiments that manifest?
7. How have imposter feelings potentially hamstrung my ambition or the scale of impact I envision?
8. Which techniques or thought processes have I initiated to tackle imposter syndrome? Are they serving their purpose? If not, what alternatives could I consider?
9. Imagining a world where I am unhindered by imposter sentiments, how would my role as a social entrepreneur evolve? What bold steps might I embrace?
10. How might I constructively remind myself of the tangible difference I've made, every time imposter feelings emerge?
11. Who are my confidants in the social impact space whom I can confide in when grappling with imposter syndrome? How might they echo back my authenticity and value?

12. How can I turn my imposter syndrome anxieties into motivation for growth and more impact?

Chapter 11

MISSION DRIFT

Sailing in Shifting Winds

This chapter traces the journey of Ahamada Houmadi, an astute social entrepreneur, who saw his venture, initially rooted in its original vision, become swept away by the turbulent currents of mission drift. Born in Comoros, Ahamada's formative years were defined by an intrinsic connection to nature and a growing awareness of the environmental challenges his island faced. Clean water and environmental conservation, he believed, were paramount to ensuring a sustainable future for his homeland.

Pooling his savings and rallying community support, Ahamada established 'Green Oasis', a social enterprise focused on sustainable water solutions and environmental conservation for Comoros' remote villages. Initially, Green Oasis grappled with issues ranging from limited resources and community hesitancy to logistical dilemmas. But with Ahamada's undying commitment, the enterprise's footprint started to take root. Green Oasis was more than a conservation initiative; it was a sanctuary where communities reconnected with nature, where local champions spearheaded green initiatives, and where preservation was the medium for future dreams.

The success of Green Oasis soon caught the attention of various entities. Philanthropists and investors approached Ahamada, offering funds to magnify the reach of his mission. One major investment originated from an international conglomerate wanting to offset its carbon footprint in Africa. This influx of capital enabled Green Oasis to expand rapidly, launching more initiatives and broadening its scope.

However, with expansion, Ahamada found his focus shifting from hands-on conservation efforts to managing investor relations and strategizing scale. These investors, equipped with their own visions of success, began directing the trajectory of Green Oasis. Eager to maintain this new growth, Ahamada found himself increasingly yielding to their preferences.

In time, Green Oasis, which had once stood for pure environmental rejuvenation, evolved into a series of commercial eco-tourism resorts. The essence transitioned from preserving ecosystems to generating tourist numbers, more resorts, and heightened profitability. The spirit of Green Oasis seemed to be fading.

During a visit to an initial project site, Ahamada anticipated warm greetings but instead faced an atmosphere of disillusionment. A village elder, who had been a stalwart supporter, expressed profound disappointment. He reminisced about Green Oasis's early days, emphasising the stark contrast between then and the commercialised entity it had become.

These poignant sentiments resonated deeply with Ahamada. He acknowledged that in pursuit of growth and profitability, Green Oasis had strayed off course. Committed to rectifying this misdirection, he reconnected with the community, redefined the organisation's goals, and made the tough decision to sever ties with investors whose vision diverged from the foundational mission.

The path to recovery was riddled with challenges. Yet, Ahamada's unwavering resolve, backed by the community and a refreshed purpose, guided Green Oasis back toward its essence. The enterprise underwent a transformation, emerging as an organisation that seamlessly married its core vision with adaptability. Ahamada championed a culture where every stakeholder, from villagers to conservationists, played a pivotal role in determining Green Oasis's path forward.

Reflecting on his experiences, Ahamada chronicled his journey in a memoir, "Winds of Change: The Odyssey of Conservation". Within its pages, he captured not just the high tides but also the tempests and times of disarray. He mused, "On this expedition, unpredictable winds might lure you into uncharted territories. Remember, the true power of your ship isn't in the grandeur of its mast, but in the fidelity of its compass."

Ahamada Houmadi's story serves as a beacon, illuminating the intricacies of navigating a purpose-driven venture amidst changing tides.

Overcoming Mission Drift
1. Define Your Social Mission Clearly. Before diving into the business aspect, articulate your social mission explicitly. This mission will be the bedrock upon which all your entrepreneurial decisions rest.

2. **Engage with Your Beneficiaries.** Regularly interact with the communities or individuals you aim to help. Their feedback can realign your venture with its primary social purpose.
3. **Selective Collaborations.** When partnering or seeking investments, prioritise those who understand and respect the social impact aspect of your venture. Their alignment with your social objectives is as important as their business acumen.
4. **Maintain a Mission-Driven Board.** Ensure your board or advisory group is composed of members passionate about your social cause. Their commitment can help the venture stay anchored to its mission.
5. **Empower Ground-Level Decision Making.** Those working directly with beneficiary communities should have a say in decisions. Their on-the-ground insights can keep strategies aligned with social goals.
6. **Diverse Impact Funding.** While it's tempting to go for large funding sources, diversify your

impact funding. This ensures one donor or investor can't unduly influence your venture away from its mission.
7. Celebrate Social Wins. Highlight and celebrate social impact milestones. It serves as a reminder of the core mission and boosts morale.
8. Future Leaders with a Heart. When thinking of succession or leadership expansion, prioritise individuals who resonate deeply with your social cause.
9. Guard Against Over-Diversification. Expanding into too many areas too quickly can dilute your focus. Ensure each expansion aligns with and doesn't distract from, your core social mission.

Mission Drift Self Reflection Questions
1. Can I see parallels between my initial zeal to impact my community and Ahamada's passion in his story?

2. Have there been moments when I felt I strayed from my foundational mission? What caused this deviation?
3. How have factors like rapid growth, funding pressures, or external expectations swayed my organisation's direction?
4. Where have I felt the push and pull between expanding my venture and staying true to its mission? How did I navigate this?
5. When confronted with feedback suggesting potential mission drift, how open was I to introspection and change?
6. During phases of significant growth or transition, how have I ensured I remain in tune with the real needs and voices of my target community?
7. Have I ever considered, like Ahamada, severing ties with stakeholders who don't resonate with my foundational vision? Have I encountered such a situation?

8. What measures or practices have I adopted to safeguard my venture against veering off its mission? Are they working?
9. Taking a cue from Ahamada's evolved vision for Brighter Horizons, how do I ensure adaptability in my venture while holding firm to its core values?
10. Reflecting on the saying, "the strength of your vessel lies not in the might of its sails, but in the integrity of its compass," what insights do I draw about my own leadership journey as a social entrepreneur?

CHAPTER 12

SUGGESTIONS ON LEVERAGING THIS BOOK

You've embarked on a journey, deep into the realm of social entrepreneurship, exploring its nuances and navigating its pitfalls. Over the previous chapters, you've learned about leadership, self-awareness, and the essentiality of avoiding self-sabotage. With all these in your mental toolkit, it's now time to take the insights and shape them into your personal roadmap.

1. Begin with Baby Steps, But Dream Big
    a. Don't rush to change everything at once.
    b. Identify 1-2 key areas for initial focus.
    c. Use reflective questions as guiding tools.
    d. Revisit our teachings on maintaining focus.
2. Embrace Compassion, Starting with Yourself.
    a. Change takes time; patience is crucial.

b. Growth is often non-linear; setbacks are learning opportunities.
   c. Treat yourself with kindness and understanding.
3. Share, Ponder, Evolve.
   a. Social entrepreneurship is personal but doesn't necessitate isolation. Leverage collective wisdom; no need to walk the path alone.
   b. Use the book as an icebreaker for team discussions or peer dialogues.
   c. Consider forming reading or reflection groups. Sharing experiences can inspire others and amplify impact.
4. Aim to be a discerning, introspective leader.
   a. Challenges are inevitable, but the journey is rewarding.
   b. Every effort is a step towards a brighter, more equitable world.
   c. Begin your transformative journey with determination.
5. Dedicate Time for Regular Introspection.

a. Set aside time for personal reflection on your journey's highs and lows.
b. Journaling or meditation can be powerful tools for self-awareness.
c. Stay attuned to your mental and emotional well-being; prioritise self-care.

Ultimately, the goal of this book is to make you an effective, self-aware leader who avoids self-sabotage and embraces continuous growth. The journey won't be easy, but it's worth undertaking. Every step you take is a step closer to becoming the change you want to see, a step towards creating a more equitable, just, and sustainable world. The road to impactful social entrepreneurship begins with a single step. Take that step today.